follow me, I am the bread of life
Love one another. Come to me...
Ask and you shall receive. I am the Light of the world
Do not be afraid, I am

BIBLE

Eli's Quiet Friend

Written by Allison Regina Gliot, FSP

Illustrated by Emily Boughton

Pauline
BOOKS & MEDIA
BOSTON

For my grandparents
and for grandparents everywhere.
Thank you for all that you are
and all that you do.

And for Sister Linda Salvatore,
who so lovingly turns words and images into books
and who would never put her own name here.

Library of Congress Control Number: 2024936425

ISBN 10: 0-8198-3172-7
ISBN 13: 978-0-8198-3172-9

Illustrated by Emily Boughton

Design by Daughters of St. Paul

Scripture quotations unless otherwise noted are from *New Revised Standard Version Bible: Catholic Edition*, copyright © 1989, 1993 National Council of the Churches of Christ in the United States of America. Used by permission. All rights reserved worldwide.

Published by Pauline Books & Media, 50 Saint Paul's Avenue, Boston, MA 02130-3491

Printed in Korea.

EQF SIPSKOGUNKYO6-26101 3172-7

www.pauline.org

Pauline Books & Media is the publishing house of the Daughters of St. Paul, an international congregation of women religious serving the Church with the communications media.

1 2 3 4 5 6 7 8 9 28 27 26 25 24

Eli was special.

He heard the sounds things make.

But he heard them all. The. Time.

He could not stop hearing them if he tried.

Sometimes, it was too much.

DAN! Turn that off and Pick up your room!
OOOOM!
vRoom
But I'm almost done with this level... Oh, not again.
BOOOM!
BANG!BANG!
GAME OVER!

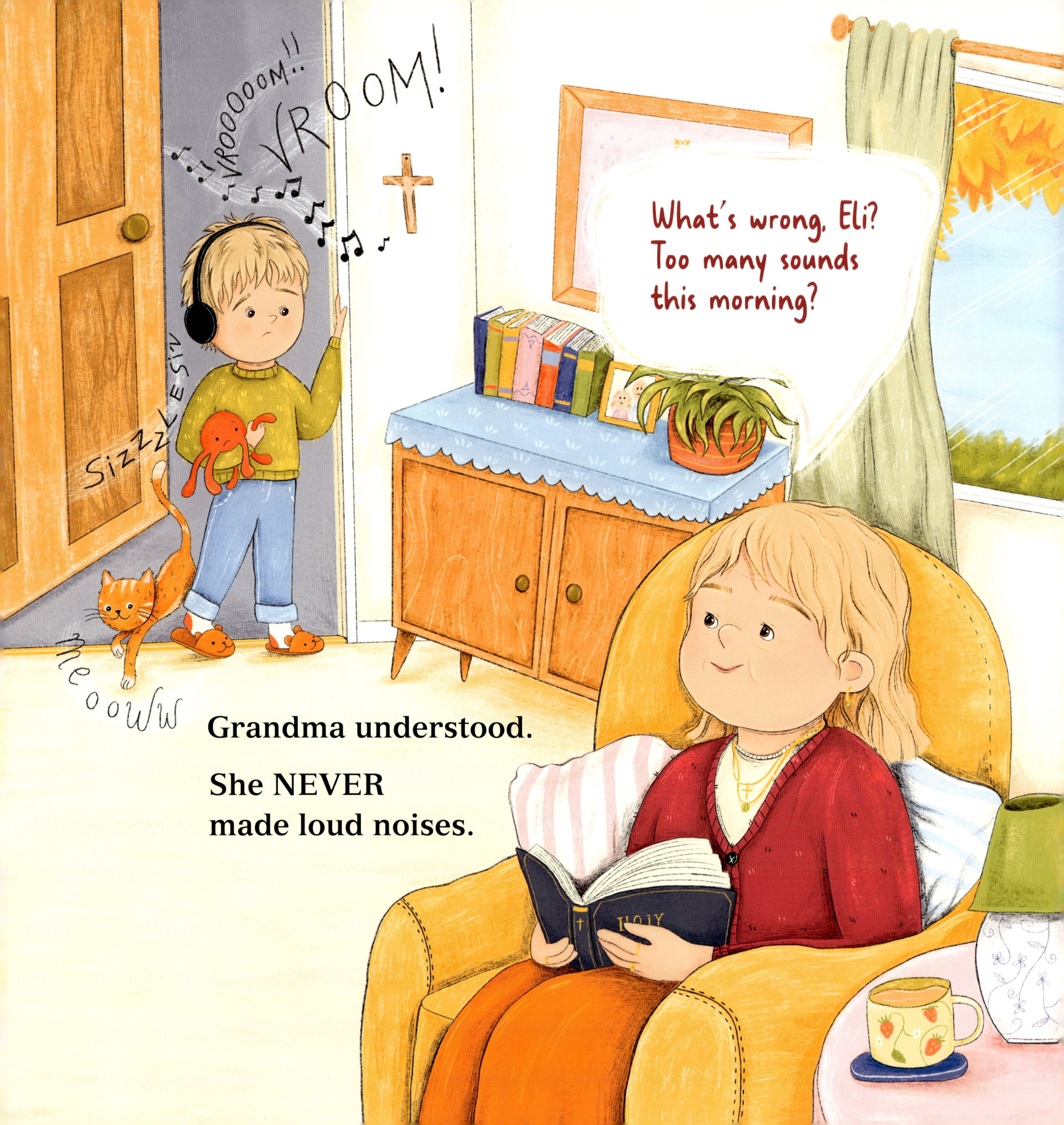

Grandma understood.

She NEVER
made loud noises.

She also told stories from her Bible that made Eli feel like he was really there.

Once, there was a man named Elijah—
just like you, Eli.

God told Elijah that he was going to pass by. So Elijah went to the mountain to wait for God.

There was a rushing wind that CRUSHED the rocks. But God was not in the wind.

Then, there was a fierce earthquake that SHOOK the ground. But God was not in the earthquake.

Then, there was a ROARING fire that burned everything up. But God was not in the fire.

Finally, there was a tiny whispering sound.

Elijah was happy because he knew God was with him.

VROOM!
VROOOM
MEOOOOW
hhhhhhshhhh
VROOOOOOM
VROOOM
VROOOOOOOM!

Oh, Eli! I'm Sorry, I didn't realize you were up already.
MEOOOW!
Eli, let's go for a walk. There is someone I want you to meet.

LA LA LA!
Good morning!
SQUEAK!
SQUEAK!
WAFFLE!
LEAVE IT!
WOOOF!
WOOOOF!
WOOOOF!
RUSTLE
RUSTLE
tweet!
tweet!
tweet!
RUSTLE
whoooooshhh
swoooosh

Eli liked walking with Grandma.

But he did not like
the city.

There were too many people making too many sounds.

The noises and people pressed on Eli until he could not stand it. He had to get away.

He ran until he found a quiet spot. Then he waited for the noise to leave him alone.

Soon, Eli heard a
new sound . . .

different from
the others.

It stirred something in his heart.

He wanted to know more.

Eli had been to church before, on Sundays when microphones were buzzing and bells were ringing and doors were slamming. But he had never been to church when it was like this.

Everything was so . . . *peaceful*.

Grandma knelt down and looked at Jesus without saying anything. Right now, she did not need to pray lots of words out loud. She was talking and listening to Jesus in her heart. Jesus could hear her, and she could hear him.

Eli watched Grandma. Why did this remind him of Elijah's story?

Suddenly, he remembered. God's voice was the quietest of all. You had to be quiet to hear him.

Quiet like the whispering sound.

Quiet like Eli.

Sh
Sh

Do not be afraid; I am with you always. I love you. Follow me. I am the Bread of Life
Love one another. Come to me.
Ask and you shall receive. I am the Light of the world

Outside, all the noises were still there. The walk back through the city was long and scary. But when they got home, Eli remembered the peace he had felt at church.

THE END.

A Prayer for Visiting Jesus

Jesus, I love you very much. I believe that the Eucharist really is you.

Help me to hear your voice and feel your love.

Teach me how to listen well so that I can know you even better. Amen.

What is the Eucharist?

The Eucharist is Jesus! Jesus is fully God *and* fully human. Isn't that amazing?! He lives in heaven, but he also wants to be with us on earth. So at every Mass he performs a special miracle to give us the Eucharist!

During the Mass, the priest says an important prayer over bread and wine. When the priest says that prayer, God turns the bread and wine into the Body and Blood of Jesus. This is called the Eucharist. The Eucharist still looks like bread and wine, but we know through faith that the Eucharist is really Jesus.

God is everywhere. He can hear you everywhere. But in the Eucharist, Jesus is with you in an extra special way. He is sitting in the very room where you are!

How can I visit Jesus in the Eucharist?

Going to Mass is an awesome way to spend time with Jesus. When the priest puts the bread and wine on the altar, pay close attention! The bread and wine are about to turn into the Body and Blood of Jesus so Jesus can be in the room with you!

Even when Mass is not going on, the Eucharist is kept in a special box called the Tabernacle, so you can still visit Jesus at church. One way to do this is through Eucharistic Adoration. That's what Eli and his grandmother did. During Eucharistic Adoration, the Eucharist is put on the altar in a special holder so that everyone can see it. People show their love and respect to Jesus in the Eucharist by praying quietly or in a group.

Do I ALWAYS have to be quiet to pray?

There are lots of ways to pray. You can do it on your own or with other people. You can say prayers out loud like the Our Father and Hail Mary. You can sing songs to God. You can read the Bible. But one very special way to pray is to talk to Jesus quietly in your heart.

You can talk to Jesus about anything! You can tell him what you are thankful for and ask him for what you need. You can tell him you love him and say you are sorry when you did something bad. Jesus listens to everything you share with him—and you don't even need to say anything out loud!

How can I hear Jesus?

Praying is not just talking to Jesus. It is also listening to him.

It is easier to hear God when we are quiet. This means trying to pay attention to Jesus and not to other things. Going to a quiet place with no distractions can help. So can taking deep breaths.

When you are quiet, think about God and how much he loves you. Sometimes, God speaks in quiet whispers, like he did to Eli. He helps you to be good and kind. He tells you how much he loves you and how he wants what is best for you.

You can also listen to God by hearing what he says in the Bible. The words of Jesus are not just meant for the people in the Bible stories. Jesus speaks them to you, too! Even though these words were written down a long time ago, Jesus may use them to say something new to you today.

Learning to hear Jesus takes practice. But the more you pray, the easier it gets!

For Grown Ups

Creating Sensory-Friendly Prayer Spaces

God created us body and soul, which means there are many ways to pray not just with our minds and hearts, but also with our bodies. Providing opportunities for children to involve their five senses in prayer without overstimulating them can help them stay grounded and focused, enabling them to engage with God on a deeper level.

One way to do this is to create a special prayer corner (or nook, den, or tent) in a room where your child feels safe. Choose a quiet spot that can be set apart and used only for that. The goal is to make a space where the child can be calm and present with God. We want to foster the child's ability to interact with God in whatever way comes most naturally, cultivating positive associations with prayer and God through the senses.

To learn more about sensory-friendly prayer spaces, and find ideas for art, environment, and interactive items that can be included, check out our resource guide at: https://connect.pauline.org/elis-quiet-friend

About the Author and the Illustrator

Sister Allison Regina Gliot, FSP, is the author of *The Book That Changed Everything*. She loves writing stories for children and teens, having fun with the sisters in her community (the Daughters of Saint Paul), and spending quiet time with her best friend: Jesus. You can find her other books at paulinestore.com.

Emily Boughton is an illustrator living and working in Hertford, U.K., specializing in children's books. When she's not creating artwork, she loves to knit and dance ballet.

receive. I am the light
do not be afraid. I am with you always. I love you follow me. I am the bread of life
Love one another. Come to me.
Ask and you shall receive. I am the light of the world
you always. I love you follow me.